The Essence of Arielle Irene Ruben:

Her Photography, Poems and Art

DEDICATION

We wish to extend a twofold dedication of these pages, with love:

First to our family, who has suffered the most unspeakable, tremendous and tragic loss, of unimaginable proportions—the death of Arielle, the youngest. Her spirit and strength still hold us. This book is a part of our healing. We hope this offering of Arielle's specialness will be a tangible memory to explore and enjoy. Our hope is that she is honored.

And, second, to the families of all those who have also experienced the loss of a child or sibling. We hope that by sharing our tribute to Arielle with the world and our seeking of peace and comfort by doing that, we will also offer a hope of healing, peace and comfort to others who grieve the loss of a child.

This book was edited and designed by
Audrey I. Russell-Kibble, Arielle's mother, and
Nora Bee Ruben, Arielle's sister
Tucson, Arizona, 2004.

To order additional copies of this book, contact:
Xlibris
1-888-795-4274
www.Xlibris.com
Orders@Xlibris.com

FOREWORD

This collection of photographs, sketches, poetry and collages was created by Arielle Irene Ruben (1985-2002). In her short life, those around her were struck by her creativity and a sense of personal style which came through in her work.

Photography class was a place where Arielle felt especially comfortable. She began snapping photos of events and people in her life—family get-togethers, friends at school, and her niece's ballet lessons. Eventually she became more deliberate, asking friends to pose as models, and mindfully looking for subject matter. As a photographer, she could show the best of others in her pictures. She had a languid, unobtrusive approach to taking pictures of her friends and family, and of herself. The softness of many of the images and use of solarization and other techniques show this sensitivity and creative personal style.

There are several unmistakable themes in Arielle's work. One major common thread is the motif of girls. Whether it was photos of girlfriends posing, her nieces' ballet class or girlish, fashion design-like sketches, she was captivated by this subject. Most of her portrayals were of a wide-eyed innocence, and a cheerfulness that she herself exuded throughout her life. She always said that it took just as much energy to be happy as sad, so she chose to be happy.

She took several trips to Mexico where she photographed barrios, people living in railroad cars and graffiti. Arielle's use of black and white film, the richness of textures she emphasized, and fine detail in this series show a new level of sophistication in her work. She had also traveled to Italy and assembled an entire album of beautiful and unique photos. Some of these she cropped and experimented with in photography class at Tucson High School, in Tucson, Arizona working with her favorite teacher, Mr. Jerry Halfman.

Arielle was also a talented artist and writer. Although many of her close friends and family did not know it, she had numerous sketchpads and journals filled with drawings, collages, poetry and prose. The pages of these journals overflow with playfulness, creativity, a natural sense of artistic knowledge, and a startling maturity. She loved magazines and made collages from them which would end up being a statement on a moral issue or a specific theme. When Arielle died there were about a hundred magazines neatly stacked in her closet. These were her media.

Some of her self portraits are eerie; especially the one of her holding up a blanket in the hallway with her head hung down to one side. She looks almost crucified. A poem in her diary was also strangely prophetic, and we have juxtaposed these two works at the end of the book.

The following pages are a sample of Arielle's photographs, poetry, and images directly from her sketchbooks. We hope that this collection will show Arielle's strong, beautiful and playful spirit, the talent that she possessed, and the value we have found in them as a memento of her.

Arielle was a person who loved to do well and have her life in order. She was accommodating and romantic and full of love for her family and friends. She was in the National Honor Society at Tucson High School with a 4.0 GPA. She was given a Scholar-Athlete award her sophomore year for getting straight A's and lettering in swimming. The next year she also joined the diving team, something she had never previously done. She planned to go to Pomona College and Stanford Medical School to become a Pediatric Surgeon. She had dreams, perspective, hopes and persistence and was planning to study and raise her SAT scores a notch.

Arielle was the youngest swim instructor and coach for the City of Tucson, at the Jesse Owens Pool. The night of her death she was so proud of her kids, who had won their swim meet. Some had written "Arielle Rocks" down the length of their arms in black marker.

All her life, Arielle had courage. She worked for Planned Parenthood of Southern Arizona when she was 15, talking to her peers at teen dances about making responsible choices. She had a tremendous sense of what was fair. When she felt that two friends were not treated with respect by other students at the private school she went to, she decided to change schools. One swim team mother told us how Arielle always had positive things to say about her child, who has a challenging disability, and how rare it was for her to ever hear such compliments about her son. A girl from her high school described how Arielle had invited her to help befriend a new boy in school, and how this girl now wished that she had gone with Arielle to participate in an offering of friendship and kindness. She enjoyed her volunteer work with the Santa Maria Soup Kitchen Interfaith Volunteers. She touched cousins, friends, classmates, teachers, teammates, and her students. At the time of her death, Arielle was just coming into her own. She was to be a senior the next year at Tucson High School. Everyone who was close to her could see and sense the maturity that seemed to appear one day.

Arielle Irene Ruben was born at home, on a ranch in Sonoita, Arizona on April 3, 1985 into her father's hands. She was a passenger in a fatal auto accident on Friday morning, June 28, 2002. She was 17 years old. A memorial has been set up in honor of Arielle. Children's Clinics for Rehabilitative Services [CCRS] in Tucson, Arizona is accepting donations in her name to be used in the dedication of a special play room. The young people whom Arielle worked with and knew have already been able to volunteer there to help with the children's care. A portion of money gained from any sales of this book will be given to that non-profit organization in her name.

We love her, and search in our hearts for the meaning she showed us in her life and in her death. We mourn the loss of all the fun and feelings that she will never now have and will miss her smile and laugh, and her, forever.

Her Family

APPRECIATION

A special thank you is extended to Jeff Neff, Jay Rochlin, Jerry Halfman, Mano Sotelo and Judy Derickson sfor their help in getting the book from a thought to production.

Commentary on the photographs, poetry and sketches
can be found at the back of the book.

[1]

[2]

[3]

6

[4]

AMR 01-21-01

ML 01-20-01

~innocence~

Just to be alive and have a bright outlook on life. Smileing and waveing at the people as you pass by. Having faith in yourself as well as other. Crying only tears of joy. Playing on swingsets without a care in the world. Picking wildflowers in the middle of spring. Singing out loud without a care in the world. Listening with a kind and open heart. Standing up for what you believe in. Praying for the health of your family and friends. Watching the stars at night while laying on your roof. Sunbathing in your backyard with your best friend. Playing in a kiddie pool with your neices and nephews. Holding hands with your mother. Getting a piggy back ride from your father. Having ribbons and flowers in your hair. Playing with a jumprope. Laughing untill you cry. Wishing on a shooting star. Screaming on the top of your lungs for your favorite band. And being thankful ~~ever~~ just for being born.

4-2-01 AR

[11]

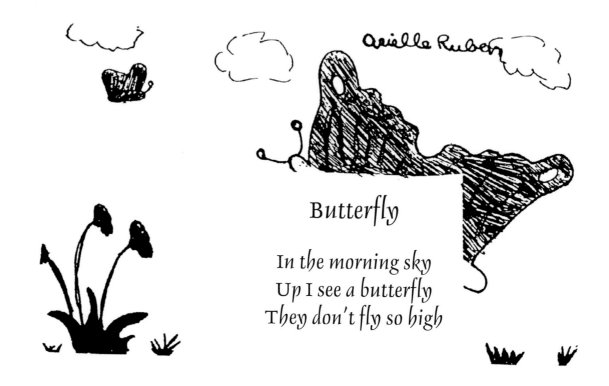

Arielle Ruben

Butterfly

In the morning sky
Up I see a butterfly
They don't fly so high

[12]

[14]

it's not sun ice

dripping
running down your chin
the smell of the park on a hot summer's day
the kids laughing and playing on the jungle gym
dripping
running down your chin
the cool feeling and sensation against your tongue
    against your tastebuds
the traffic speeding by on a busy afternoon
dripping
running down your face
the flavors melt in your mouth
sweating by the hot sun
dripping
running down your face
the ducks swimming in the lake
the fountain shooting up
the kids throwing bread
dripping
running down your face
the feel of the fresh cut grass upon
    your naked feet
the rays of the sun melting your treat
eat fast
dripping
running down your face
gone

[15]

[16]

[1

[18]

18

[19]

[20]

Flowers

The buds open up,
For a new day,
Now they're smelling nice.

Nistly Mystified

under the ulloff tree
I swing on a swig
Round goes the blistful world around me
Budoff songs flow in the mistiful air
while the liftnee birds lang along
calling of the rash-ume man
who plays his darman while he
walks through the clowts
Diddle-daddle
bing-bong
click-clack
    don't you hear the ishloff of
    the kling-klang band?
    listen niftly and you will hear
    them again
tick-tack
shing-shang
par-poo
lis-lass
    Oh kling-klang band come
play your stam tonight.

[22]

[23]

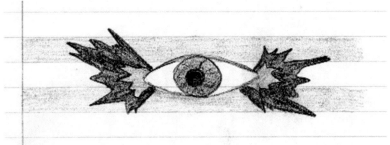

You and Me

As the sun goes down the stars come out,
to feel the rain of the nice chilling drought.

As the moon rises out of the dusk up ahead.

The glow of the sun is overcome by the light of the moon, in the dune,
in the dusk, the flowers close to save their sweet musk.

For a new day will come and there will be,
some sweet music for just you and me.

[24]

A long time ago, actually it wasn't that long ago, I met someone who would leave my life as quickly as he had entered. In a short while after meeting him I began to know him, or at least I thought I knew him. He was sweet, sensitive, and very sexy. Everything I could ever want, But he was also not the person I once thought he was. We shared a lot with eachother. I wanted our relationship never to end. We hung out at the park, watched movies, and watched the sunset. We held hands and just talked. He was very special to me. He asked me to trust him and eventually I did. He made me promises that he did not intend   to keep. They did not all come true. I wish-   -ed on shooting stars and had many   dreams about him. I never thought that

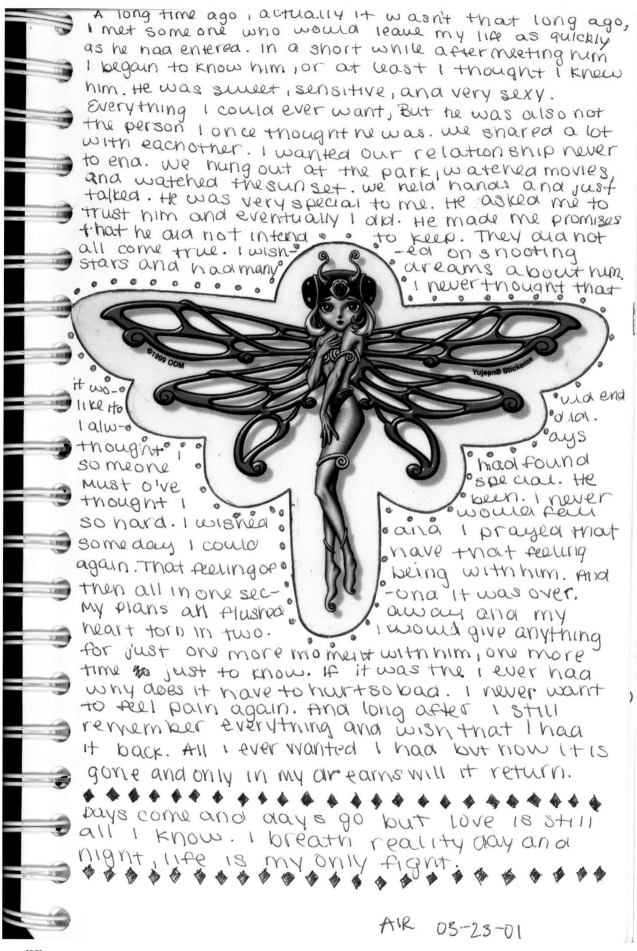

©1999 ODM

Yujean® Stickeme

it wo-
uld end
like to
d.lol.
I alw-
ays
thought I
had found
someone
special. He
must o've
been. I never
thought I
would fall
so hard. I wished
and I prayed that
someday I could
have that feeling
again. That feeling of
being with him. And
then all in one sec-
-ond it was over.
My plans all flushed
away and my
heart torn in two.
I would give anything
for just one more moment with him, one more
time so just to know. If it was the I ever had
why does it have to hurt so bad. I never want
to feel pain again. And long after I still
remember everything and wish that I had
it back. All I ever wanted I had but now it is
gone and only in my dreams will it return.
◆◆◆◆◆◆◆◆◆◆◆◆◆◆◆◆◆◆◆◆◆◆◆
Days come and days go but love is still
all I know. I breath reality day and
night, life is my only fight.
◆◆◆◆◆◆◆◆◆◆◆◆◆◆◆◆◆◆◆◆◆

AIR   05-23-01

[26]

[27]

[28]

WAR

A statue, An invasion,
A gift, no.

It is hate that leads to war,
war that leads to death,
death that leads to agony and despair.

A trick, An underworld,
A life to kill.

Emotions that you can not control,
breathing inside of you,
like a red rose in your breast.

A family, A friend,
A sin that was made.

War over a woman,
beautiful as can be.
No more hate, No more anger.

A heart, A soul,
An end.

[29]

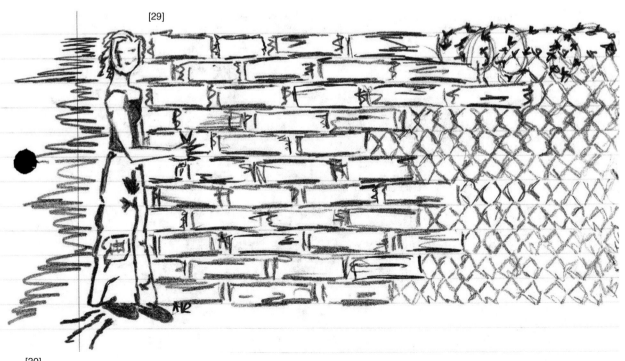

[30]

[31]

[32]

[33]

PATHS

Don't change the paths of life,

let it grow,

let it be for the heavens, the earth,

but mostly the sea.

[34]

[35]

[36]

CIRCLE OF LIFE

Love the rain that fills the ocean blue.
Don't let him go for he is your dinner.
Calm him down for he must care.
Make the most of every day.
For this is the circle of life.

[37]

[38]

[39]

Not a lock or a coin
Not a lock or a coinNot a lock or a coin I Not a lock or a coinI give you a key
It is the light of the day
It promises adventures
　　like the ones in the story books
Here is a present
It will open doors
　　like a magic sword
I am trying to be helpful
　　not a pest
I give to you a key
　　TAKE IT!!
Not a cloud or a star
I give to you a dream
It is a ring of grass
It promises your own wonder of hope
　　like the charity of love
Here please have it
It will bring you love
　　like the birds in the sky
I am trying to share my dreams
Not an unpeaceful thought
I give you a dream
It's mine
Please take it

[40]

[41]

My Life

I live my life on the rocks
I let the candlelight abide
I sing songs to the rhythm of the crashing
    waves against the shore
I grow strong with each current
I fear day with each new sun
I have hope that someone will find me
    in this long, deep, dark cave of mine
I am trapped in by squid and crayfish
My only memories are of fear
My father sent me here
My mother thinks I'm dead
I am alone in a cave
I am trapped from life

[43]

GAZING

Strive! Take a deep breath and dive!

A colorful world of coral and fish to gaze upon,

right then and there, what do you see?

A wonderful world under the sea.

[44]

[45]

Once we wished upon a star
but never knew we'd get so far.
Once we cried for no reason at all
but little did we know we wouldn't fall.
Once we had a friend to care
but didn't know he was never there.
Once we thought of horrible things
but got the courage to spread our wings.
Once we angered and sought to fight
but didn't notice the peacefulness of that night.
Once we hoped that day would come
but we didn't know what had to be done.
Once we laughed ourselves to tears
but never knew it wouldn't calm our fears.
Once we cared but now we don't
but we didn't realize that we said "we won't".
Once we had a dream of death
now you can lay me down to rest.

[46]

Once we wished upon a star,
but never knew we'd get so far.
Once we cried for no reason at all
but little did we know we wouldn't fall
Once we had a friend to care
but didn't know he was never there
Once we thought of horrible things
but got the courage to spread our win
Once we angered and sought to fight
but didn't notice the peacefulness of that night.
Once we hoped that day would come
but we didn't know what had to be done
Once we laughed ourselves to tears
but never knew it wouldn't calm our fears
Once we cared but now we dont
but we didn't realize that we said "we wont"
Once we had a dream of death
now you can layme down to rest.

[47]

I turn
but nothing
but an image
that's not even there
I stare
and wait
for a smile of emptiness
And then
I fall
when I see
what has begun
a new one
I spin
in dizziness
I crash
into the empty arms of
nobody
I long
to feel that touch
of tenderness
and the stars
twirl
as my soul
raises out of my chest
just to land on the ground
and be walked upon
not even seen
no one even cares
just me
melting into
eternity

[49]

[50]

COMMENTARY ON THE PHOTOGRAPHS, POETRY AND SKETCHES

COVER: This portrait of Arielle was framed and given to her mother for Mother's Day. The interesting thing about it is the way the ragged upper edges, torn from a Polaroid, make their own kind of frame around her face. She loved this portrait.

FRONT PIECE: This self portrait was taken with a blue filter on her Pentax 28-80 with her holding an umbrella she got in Chinatown in San Francisco, posing in front of her bedroom dressing mirror. The mirror is in the center of the closet door, which is decorated with a collage of magazine cutouts, stickers, and commentary.

[1] Sarena is very photogenic and Arielle captured her beauty in an extensive portfolio. Sarena used some of these for her senior portraits at Tucson High School.

[2] This sketchbook rendition of girls at a coffee shop, whispering, languishing, flirting shows the essence of what was important to this teenage girl.

[3][4] Mariah was posed by Arielle, and just as in the sketches [2][3], her hand is to her face and she has closed lips.

[5][6][7] Sketches of girls in prom dresses and curly hair and casual wear with detailed borders, brightened with colored pencils, these unique drawings were sketched while sitting cross-legged on her bed.

[8] Arielle's sister Ayla was photographed at the mirrored, upside down, pyramid bank building at the crossroads of Speedway and Wilmot in Tucson, Arizona.

[9] This bit of prose was read at Arielle's funeral service by Rabbi Tom Loucheim.

[10] Arielle's niece Sage is enthralled by her first birthday cake and the timing was perfect for the essence of the mood. The hands placed in the center of the photograph shows the true focus of the topic.

[11] Arielle's niece Rhiannon making cookies from homemade play dough for her second birthday.

[12] The Butterfly haiku and sketch were published in the St. Gregory Middle School Literary Magazine.

[13] Arielle took her niece Darbe out for a walk and perched her on the fire hydrant to take her picture in black and white. She later, delicately, hand colored the photograph.

[14] Arizpe is a beautiful child whose natural pose in the grass was caught on film.

[15] "its not sun ice" was composed during her Emily Dickinson phase of poetry composition. No punctuation or capitals were deemed necessary, and this lack of barriers helps the ice cream along as it runs down your face.

[16] Sage in goggles at the pool is irresistible, and Arielle captures her glee.

[17][18][19] Rhiannon's first ballet recital was photographed from start to finish by Arielle. Later she played with some of the film, first solarizing a shot and then mounting and staining it. This finished piece is very cute at 5"X6". The mounted version of the photograph is lightly sepia toned.

[20] The back of the original mounted photograph is labeled "glass roses".

[21] The Flowers haiku.

[22] "Nistly Mystified" has a note from Arielle's teacher which states,'This was a lot of fun to read—creatively coined words'.

[23] An eye drawing found on a piece of school notebook paper.

[24] Her romantic and eternally optimistic side is evident in the poem "You and me".

[25] A sticker and a note to herself is how she coped with the heartache of young love.

[26] This collage was done in one of her sketch books. The pink fish background is surrounded by love, hearts, kisses. Nothing is random. The perfume bottle is heart shaped on top, the edging placed to frame the entirety.

[27] Ashley's family is from Nigeria. Arielle loved the Mgbulu family. The solarization of this photograph of Ashley's hand was done in several different motifs and also enlarged to poster size for a show and she titled it, "Strength". She received a recognition for it.

[28] Priscilla's hands are held together but it is not altogether known what the item is.

[29] Many of her poems, such as this one, were simply found on a computer disc.

[30] Another sketch done on notebook paper.

[31] A photograph of a wall in a barrio showing both street art and graffiti. She let it stand on its own, as a complete work, without having us look at the context around it.

[32][33] In Italy she photographed extensively.

[34] This poem was found among a collection titled, "Sea".

[35] Another photograph from Italy.

[36] Photographed at the island of Capri.

[37] Another poem from the "Sea" collection.

[38] Another photograph from Italy.

[39] A good example of her playfulness is shown here. She originally shot the photograph of the Leaning Tower of Pisa by turning the camera slightly to 'straighten it up', and then later when working with her film in the darkroom she tilted it back again, and so there are several variations printed up.

[40] Another poem in the genre of Emily Dickinson, whom she loved to read.

[41] On notebook paper, this sketch and note to herself expresses heartache again.

[42] Self portrait in the hallway, using a door as the background, holding a cloth softly, slightly out of focus, serious, almost a bit sad, this tender photograph is rich.

[43] Another poem from the Emily Dickinson time, no punctuation, melancholy. Her teacher's comment on the original states, "This is so sad. Strong poem".

[44] Another poem from the "Sea" collection.

[45] The photograph of Arielle is of her actually diving during a swim meet, which she cut out and superimposed onto the computer generated picture with a dramatic result.

[46][47] This poem is presented both printed and in its original handwritten version where it is easy to see her thought process because of the use of two different colors of ink. The first few lines, the succession of 'Once's' and the last lines were written first and the remainder added later. An eerie predilection of death is apparent.

[48] More experimentation with the cloth, the door, movement with the shutter open.

[49] This poem portrays an eerie and ironic reminder of how Arielle died. The spin, the crash, the soul raising out of her lends itself to imagining the fatal auto accident in which she died. It was actually found in her diary, and was written at a time when she was having hurt feelings over the disappointment of a potential boyfriend letting her down. She, however, had high standards and refused to be stood up, even once, and always encouraged her friends to have those same high standards and opinions of themselves.

[50] This sensitive self portrait caused us all to take pause and consider:
the pose, almost crucified, the slightly out of focus depiction, her beauty and strength.

[51] BACK PIECE: From the Barrio series: plants potted in cans in an alleyway.

[52] BACK COVER: Self portrait in front of her mirror and collaged door.

Printed in the United States
By Bookmasters